The Adventure of Wiping

The Adventure of Wiping

WRITTEN BY **SAMUEL ELKHOURY**

ILLUSTRATED BY **LAUREN ZURCHER**

SPRING CEDARS®

First edition, 2021

Illustrations and book cover by Lauren Zurcher
Book design by Spring Cedars

ISBN 978-1-950484-13-3 (paperback)

Published by Spring Cedars LLC
Denver, Colorado
info@springcedars.com
springcedars.com

ALL AROUND THE PLANET, DOESN'T MATTER THE TIME,
THEY COULD BE RUNNING, OR RESTING, OR PLAYING
WITH SLIME.

THEIR BODIES FREEZE,
THEIR FACES GET
DROOPY,
THEY FARTED ALL THEY
COULD, IT'S TIME TO
POOPY.

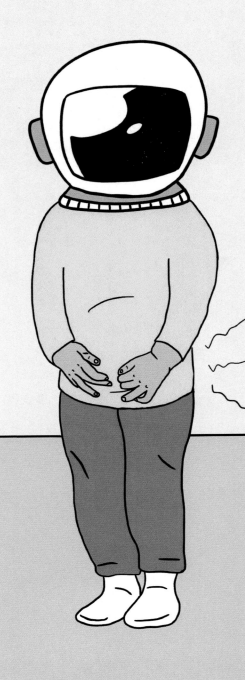

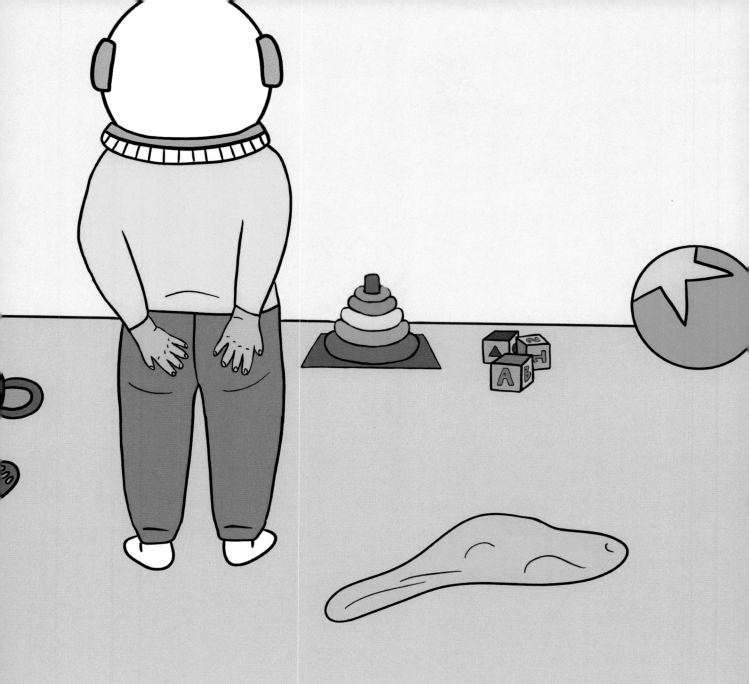

HAND ON THE BUTT, RUMBLING IN THE TUMMY,
ABOUT TO LAUNCH, WARNING DADDY OR MOMMY.

"HURRY, HURRY, BE QUICK ON YOUR
FEET,
HEAD TO THE SPACESHIP AND TAKE
YOUR SEAT."

FINALLY THERE, NO TIME TO CLOSE THE DOOR,
READY FOR BLAST-OFF, PANTS HIT THE FLOOR.

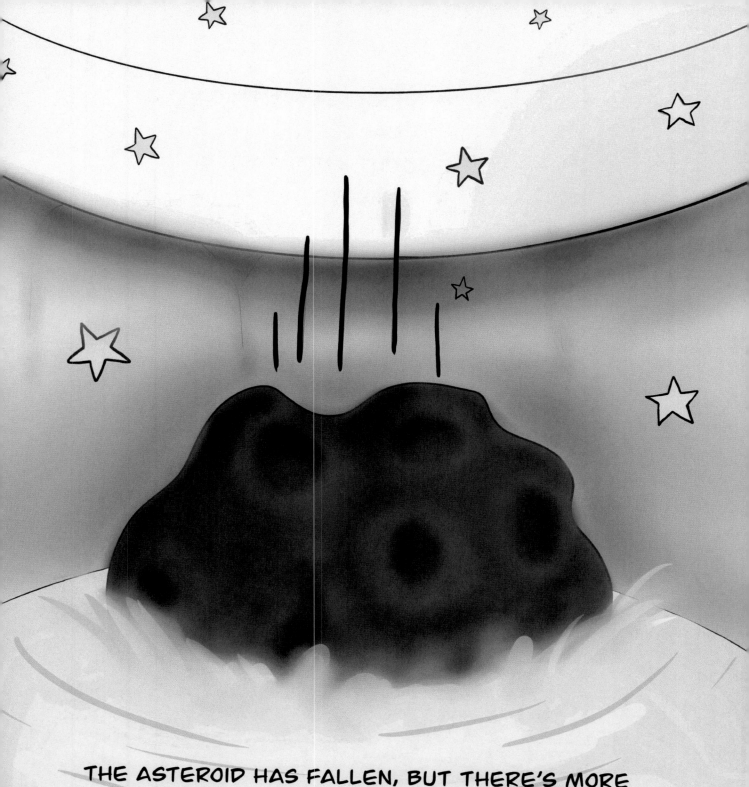

THE ASTEROID HAS FALLEN, BUT THERE'S MORE
TO TELL,
AND WE'RE NOT ONLY TALKING ABOUT THE
SMELL.

"YOU HAVE TO TAKE IT SLOW, THIS IS NO RACE,
BE LIKE A SCOUT AND LEAVE NO TRACE."

8

"LISTEN UP CREW, LET'S PLAN THE ATTACK, YOU CAN APPROACH FROM THE FRONT OR THE BACK."

"KEEP IN MIND, YOU'LL NEED A SMOOTH LANDING, GIVE A LITTLE SHAKE TO CLEAR THE LAST ONES STANDING."

"FOR THE NEXT STEP WE MUST BE VERY CLEAR, ALWAYS WIPE AWAY, TOWARD THE REAR."

"START WITH TWO SHEETS, MAKE SURE TO COVER THE HAND, GO REAL SLOW AS YOU NAVIGATE THE LAND."

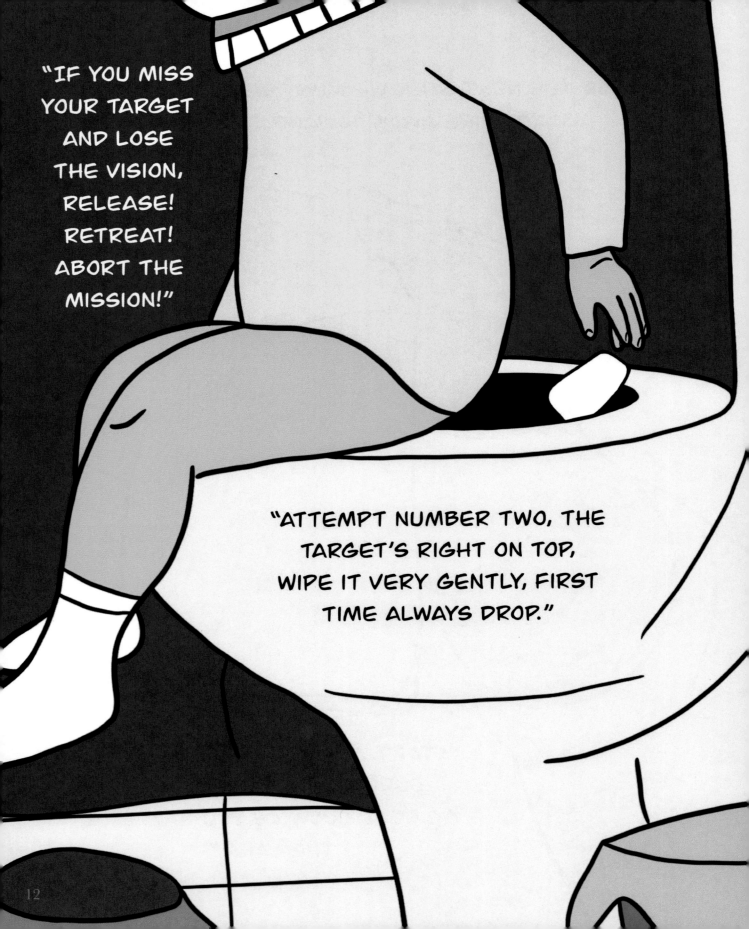

"YOU ACCOMPLISHED THE MISSION, NOW YOU'RE ALL CLEAN,
YOU KNOW HOW TO WIPE, LET'S MAKE THIS A ROUTINE."

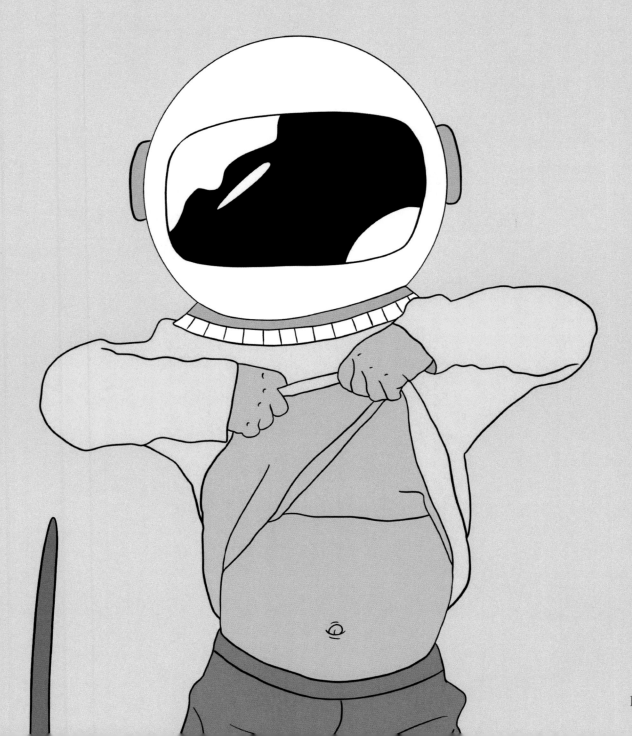

THE ADVENTURE OF WIPING IS DEFINITELY INHERENT,
"NOW WE HAVE A CLOGGER, CALL OUT FOR YOUR PARENT."

About the Author

Samuel Elkhoury is originally from Lebanon. He grew up traveling the world since his father worked for the United Nations. At the age of 19, Samuel moved to the United States to study and graduated with a B.S. in Computer Science from Georgia State University. He currently lives in Atlanta with his wife and two sons, igniting both sides of his brain as a software engineer and creative writer.

About the Illustrator

Lauren Zurcher began her journey as an illustrator at the age of six drawing and writing in her journal about family vacations across the world. Growing up she attended bilingual schools where classes were taught in both English and French. She lives in Colorado and loves bringing stories to life with colorful and playful visuals. Visit bylaurenzurcher.com for more.